How To Succeed In Your

First Job

from the Get Ahead of the Pack series

By Serena De Maio and Anna Lundberg

First edition

ISBN: 978-1527200371

Wolf Leaders Academy is a training organisation that unleashes the potential of ambitious and self-motivated individuals, arming them with the tools and skills they need to fast-track their career. We are creating a global community of Wolf Leaders by offering courses on the most important skills of an alpha – from strategic thinking and the power of influence to managing your career and your boss, from effective project management to engaging and exciting your multi-functional team.

PREFACE

It is not an exaggeration to say that my first year in the corporate world was a complete failure. Compared to my most brilliant colleagues, my lack of leadership skills and work ethic slowed the progress of my career by at least two years. And as if that wasn't damaging enough, the mistakes I made in those early days established a negative image in the minds of more senior colleagues, an image that took me years to erase.

Arriving late at meetings? Check. Not taking notes? Check. Pissing off my boss? Check, check, check! So was that whole first year wasted? Not at all.

During those first months, I learned the hard way what it takes to succeed. I draw your attention to the word *learned* because, although there are some rare 'naturals', most of us are not born as ready-made leaders – but we can thrive with the right guidance. Unfortunately in my case, at the time I didn't have that guidance. Or maybe I was deaf to it, overwhelmed as I was by work.

Fast forward 10 years, and I am now responsible for the success of 10 brands in 40 markets, generating 250 million euro in retail sales, and managing 10+ people. I work closely with junior managers and I can't help but observe that most of them make the same mistakes that I did. In this book you will find a selection of the most important advice and techniques that I share with them to get their careers off to a flying start. I have no doubt it will help you too to leap well ahead of the pack and have a memorable start in the corporate wilderness of your new job.

- Serena, Co-Trainer at Wolf Leaders Academy
Geneva, June 2016

When I started as an Assistant Brand Manager in the perfume department at Procter & Gamble, I knew nothing about marketing, perfume, or the company itself; yet somehow I thought I could, or should, manage all by myself. So I didn't ask for support, I didn't ask any questions, and I just got on with it. Impressive? Or just plain stupid?

Unlike Serena, I had a flying start and excelled from the beginning. I was lucky to have a supportive boss, I absorbed everything like a sponge, and most of all I delivered all my projects successfully through sheer grit. Now, ten years later, I'm applying the leadership skills I've developed and the knowledge I've accumulated as an independent consultant and coach, and I'm incredibly grateful for everything I've learned that makes me successful today. It would all have been a lot less painful, though, if I had had access to these insights and techniques back when I started!

It's in the individual's but also the company's interest to get new hires up to speed as quickly as possible. Corporate training programmes are too slow, too longwinded or, frankly, too corporate to get the key points across in that first critical period. It's our hope that Wolf Leaders Academy can fill that gap by bringing comprehensive but straightforward tips and techniques directly to you as you embark on your career; starting with *How to Succeed in Your First Job*.

- Anna, Co-Trainer at Wolf Leaders Academy
London, June 2016

CONTENTS

INTRODUCTION

So you want to be a Wolf Leader?

Did you know that wolf pups are born blind and deaf? They must learn to crawl before they can stand and walk, they are first fed by their mother and must learn from the adults before they can hunt for themselves, they must develop their physical strength and maturity. Fewer than half of the pups born in the wild will survive into adulthood, and most of those who do survive will live their lives as subordinates rather than alpha leaders.

And it's 'survival of the fittest' in the corporate wilderness as well. Far too many newly hired managers quit their jobs within the first months, with many more failing to meet expectations in their early years in the company. It's our belief that these numbers can be greatly reduced by setting clear expectations at the start and by providing proper coaching and support to help you not just to survive but to thrive in this new environment.

In *How To Succeed in Your First Job*, you'll learn how to make a good impression from day one, how to manage expectations and get your boss on your side, how to stay on top of your workload, how to apply your strategic thinking, how to communicate effectively, and how to engage the broader multi-functional team towards a common vision. Mastering these techniques will help you shine but just as importantly it will help you to feel that you're really doing meaningful work – and having fun while you're doing it.

We wrote this book to bring together all the advice that we wish we had had when we started out in our first jobs. Although it's too late for us, we're thrilled to be able to offer you the chance to get access to all this wisdom at this early point in your career! In each chapter, we give our top tips and techniques for you to master a particular aspect of corporate management and leadership skills, illustrated with personal insights from senior directors and consultants as well as junior managers whose first months are still fresh in their minds. Some chapters include an additional 'Wolf tool' and you'll also have special access to bonus content available to download from the website.

We believe in the insights and tips that we're sharing in this book, derived from many decades of accumulated experience in the corporate world. If you take on board these lessons and apply them in your work environment, we are confident that you will see the impact on your projects as well as in the positive feedback you'll be getting from your boss and from your team.

So what makes a wolf rise in the ranks of the pack and become an alpha? What makes a true Wolf Leader? Read on to discover *How to Succeed in Your First Job...*

CHAPTER 1: ESTABLISHING YOURSELF IN THE PACK

Earning respect from day one

CHAPTER 1: ESTABLISHING YOURSELF IN THE PACK

Earning respect from day one

Congratulations on your new job! You've clearly impressed and you've been given a chance to show everyone what you're capable of. But now that you're in, you have to realise that you're starting from a blank slate. You may have been a superstar with your teachers and professors but here you're just one in the crowd; by definition, 90% of you will no longer be in the top 10%! Be aware of the signals that you are sending from your very first day, and think of the impression you want to give as to who you are and what you stand for. A reputation is earned, and takes time; the coming days and months will be critical.

1. Be ready to learn.

The bias of a lot of people in senior management will be that the younger generation is arrogant and know-it-all, and this is only made worse by your gung-ho attitude during your very first days in the office. Enthusiasm and confidence will get you a long way, but you need to understand the framework in which you're operating before you bring on the revolution. Keep your eyes and ears open and, above all, keep an open mind as you learn everything you can about this new environment. Even new CEOs have been known to spend as long as six months simply learning before they start taking any action at all – and, in case you've forgotten, you've got a few years to go until you reach that level!

> *"Learn, learn, learn! In the first 3-6 months, learn as much as you can about the new company and its business, get to know as many people as possible and learn who are the key influencers. Make sure you try to understand first,*

before aiming to be understood."

- Christian Bulla, Head of Marketing at Ravensburger
16 YEARS OF EXPERIENCE

"Be curious. Ask questions. Listen actively and learn fast. That means doing your homework, asking intelligent questions and being genuinely interested in your co-workers, colleagues, direct reports and your superiors. You should seek to: (i) understand what is expected from you and how your performance will be measured and (ii) discover how you can add value to your organisation and your team.

The first comes from asking smart questions and defining objectives clearly and quickly. The second comes from listening and patiently observing the ways things are done and identifying 'pain points' within the organisation. Knowing when to speak up with a suggestion and when to keep quiet is an art and a skill."

- Tom O'Brien, Managing Director & Partner at Lovebite, Client Service Director at LOLA Mullen Lowe
32 YEARS OF EXPERIENCE

"When a new hire is joining the company, the first priority should be to learn (i) the organisation culture, (ii) the decision-making process and (iii) the business and its objectives. Be curious, ask questions, connect the dots, quickly understand the business challenges, engage and connect with key people, and execute tasks with excellence."

- Eric Dekoninck, Head of Global Brand & Marketing, Private Fundraising & Partnership at UNICEF
15 YEARS OF EXPERIENCE

"Focus more on your speed of development and learning than on how you are perceived by others. Development over prestige. Don't focus too much on trying to be good immediately instead of just learning really fast. It sounds like a paradox but it really isn't."

- **Christopher Engman, Founder & Head of Vendemore**
30 YEARS OF EXPERIENCE

"The quality of your learning is directly proportional to your personal investment – so you must get involved, ask the right questions, listen to understand, experience things first hand, connect with more senior people for their experiences, mingle with more junior people to get theirs.

Once you feel you have acquired this understanding, then please, be my guest: re-invent, improve, test, break, and challenge the rulebooks! You will see that your interventions will be finer, more educated, more impactful, and more sustainable thanks to this initial investment in learning first."

- **Kenny Kerswell, Senior Consultant at Kinetic Consulting**
15 YEARS OF EXPERIENCE

2. Take notes.

You should be taking copious notes in all your meetings, whether in your one-to-one with your boss or in a large presentation with senior management. You may think you'll remember what you've discussed but most probably you won't. Besides that, it's about the impression you're giving to management: taking notes shows that you're engaged and willing to learn. That being said, this is not an exercise in dictation, it's not about writing down every word everyone says: you need to be selective and note down the key facts, points on which you should be following up, people to talk to, action steps that you should be taking after the meeting. You can also jot down thoughts and questions that arise, as well as any acronyms or terms you didn't understand so that you can ask someone later on.

> *"Arrogance is the kiss of death. Try to strike that right balance of confidence and humility, speaking and truly listening."*
>
> **- Pauline Manos, Independent Consultant, Trainer & Mentor**
> **24 YEARS OF EXPERIENCE**

3. Work your arse off.

During your first year, you're going to have to work. Hard. That may not be what you wanted to hear, but it's the reality if you want to do well. Work-life balance is incredibly important, and it's something that we take very seriously at Wolf Leaders Academy – but that doesn't change the fact that you'll need to knuckle down now and get on with it. There may be more work than life for a while…

> *"I can't think of a time when I did not work incredibly hard as I joined a new company. The combination of the new challenge, mental freshness, and a steep learning curve has typically resulted in grinding out 12-to-14-hour days and checking email after 10pm almost every day (not to mention the weekends). Although this is not sustainable over time (beware of burnouts!), there is an appealing adrenaline-like kick to this phase."*
>
> **- Kenny Kerswell, Senior Consultant at Kinetic Consulting**
> **15 YEARS OF EXPERIENCE**

"I did work hard and long hours, especially at the beginning. I did it because I loved what I was doing, I enjoyed the people I was with, and I was learning a lot; I never did that just for the sake of a career. Working hard and long hours is worth it only if you enjoy what you are doing... it is never worth it only for a career."

- Vincenzo Carrara, Director, Author, Entrepreneur
15 YEARS OF EXPERIENCE

4. Be among the first in the office... but don't be the last.

Staying late every night is a sign that you can't manage your time and workload effectively, and that you're getting bogged down in trivial details and tasks. If you have something you want to continue working on, then make sure you note it down so that you start on that first thing the next day. If you've got 'flow' and you want to keep working late into the night, take your laptop home and work in the evening, saving any emails to send the next morning when you're back in the office. There may, of course, be times when you have a big project or presentation with an urgent deadline and your boss, and your team, will be counting on you to put in those extra hours to make it a success – but it shouldn't be a daily occurrence.

"I wish I had known that you cannot do everything! When I started I was trying to nail every priority, which meant back then working from 4am to 8pm. I realised that I was reaching the point of exhaustion for results that were not necessarily being valued by management. It took me more than a year to let some objectives go by understanding and aligning with my manager what were the three 'no-miss' priorities. It allowed me to perform better on the core priorities – and got me promoted!"

17

- Sales Manager at Procter & Gamble
4 YEARS OF EXPERIENCE

5. Get a watch, and use it.

Turning up late to meetings is disrespectful to your managers and to your colleagues, and again shows that you are not in control of your workload or your agenda. This is all the more critical if it's your meeting, when it's your responsibility to be there on time and to gather the team and management - don't ever make them come and look for you! Start on time, keep the discussion focused on the desired outcome of the meeting, and make sure you don't run over. *[See also **Rule 42: Own your meetings**, page 68]*

> *"One of the biggest mistakes I've seen a new hire is to be late to their 1-on-1 meetings, as well as not taking notes. It sounds small but unfortunately this kind of behaviour will gain you negative 'share of mind'."*

- Dimitris Papalexopoulos, Head of EMEA Sales Development at Google
9 YEARS OF EXPERIENCE

6. Dress professionally.

People will make up their minds in the first seconds of meeting you so consider the impression you're giving. Female wolves listen up: there's nothing wrong with dressing fashionably, but save the ripped jeans and low-cut top for the weekend – dressing that way will only distract both men and women from whatever you're actually trying to communicate. Male wolves: please don't wear super-tight or see-through shirts with your chest hair on display, or have your boxers hanging out. It's not a good look. Really.

WOLF LEADER TIP: APPEARANCE MATTERS

You may disagree on principle, but the fact remains that appearance is still an important consideration in a professional work environment. If you still need convincing:

*44% of managers are less likely to promote someone who wears provocative clothing to work
*43% are less likely to promote someone who wears wrinkled clothes
*27% are less likely to promote someone who dressed too casually for the workplace

Source: http://www.trendhunter.com/trends/promotion-factors

Joanna Gaudoin, Personal and Corporate Image Expert at Inside Out, elaborates:

"If you had gone into most office environments 30 years ago, there would have been a very 'uniform' dress code. Nowadays, there is a lot more variety, even within sectors and certainly between sectors. Whilst this can make dressing for work challenging for some, it does provide the opportunity to show more personality, make ourselves more positively memorable, as well as feeling more like ourselves, which is important to perform to the best of our ability.

The key element is appropriateness. It's vital to think about your day – what will you be doing? Is there more of a need to be authoritative or approachable? What meetings do you have planned? Importantly, who are they with? You need to think about how the people you are meeting will be dressed and what their expectation of you is. They would expect a lawyer to be dressed differently to a media planner!

It's not just about the actual 'dress code' level itself but how you use colour, style of clothing and specifics of clothing and accessories. In some roles or sectors, there might be a very different look required even within the same week. Remember too that details count: the smartest suit can be undermined by dirty shoes and messy hair! Equally, casual dress should never mean messy in a professional context.

It's important for managers to remember they are role models for others. What do you want to communicate? What do you want to be remembered for? Whilst clothes shouldn't be the key point of memorability, positive professional dress means people will engage with your expertise and experience more readily and remember you for them!"

7. Look after yourself.

The rule of the survival of the fittest applies in the corporate world as in the wild, and staying physically fit and healthy will help you endure the long working hours and keep your energy up. Make sure that you get your 7-8 hours of sleep, drink plenty of water, go running, train at the gym, or do whatever it is you like to do to keep fit. You'll feel stronger and more confident, and be more able to stay on top of your workload than if you're running on Red Bull and Snickers.

"In my first two years of work, I gained 17 kilos. I worked late all the time, neglected my body and ate badly. For the first time I had money to buy take-away food every day and I had stopped exercising after college. Don't make the same mistake! Work-life balance is vital for your success at work and outside of it. Work smart so you don't have to work so hard.

Leaving work late all the time means you are inefficient, nothing else. Work is a never-ending process, it can never be complete so pick what is most important first and do that during the hours you are paid for."

- Dylan van Vuuren, Assistant Brand Manager at Procter & Gamble
4 YEARS OF EXPERIENCE

"A junior manager should never underestimate the importance of mental and physical energy required to be a great leader and great individual. 'Work hard, play hard' comes with training and an ability to rest mentally and physically. Finding the right personal balance is critical, as it will help in the long run versus focusing on the short term."

- Eric Dekoninck, Head of Global Brand & Marketing, Private Fundraising & Partnership at UNICEF
15 YEARS OF EXPERIENCE

Joanna Gaudoin, Personal and Corporate Image Expert at Inside Out, advises:

"If you think of an artist, he needs a good canvas to create a great painting. Think of your body as a canvas. Whilst it's not about being perfect, you will look your best when you are in good health – that means not having dark circles from tiredness, and sallow skin from poor diet and lack of fresh air, to name a couple. Being at a healthy weight is important too, for health and so that clothes fit well and you feel confident about yourself. Inner confidence shows externally! A good diet and exercise also help the mind.

Small changes can make all the difference – get off a stop early, park the car slightly further away, take the stairs

> not the lift, swap that chocolate bar for an apple or eat less of it than you normally would!"

8. No zob in job! As the French say. *(No sex at work!)*

Don't play around in the office. It may feel like a university campus but remember that you might soon have to work closely with somebody you never wanted to see again... Of course things are bound to happen, but at least be discreet and keep it out of the office. Likewise, be a little wary at office parties and events. By all means enjoy yourself but don't get so drunk that you turn up at work with a stinking hangover the next day, and don't put yourself in a situation where you only discover at the coffee machine what embarrassing things you got up to the night before in front of your Vice President...

9. Don't gossip.

Office life can at times feel like reality TV. We're human beings, and personal interaction is important to understanding each other and getting the work done. But don't engage in idle gossip, don't spread rumours that may or may not be true, and don't bitch behind someone's back. It makes you look bad and will make people less likely to trust you in the future, both personally and professionally – and trust is critical in a work environment. Also remember: if someone is happy to gossip with you, they're probably going to gossip about you as well, so keep that in mind before you share what's on your mind.

> *"The biggest mistake a new hire can make is to get embroiled in any office politics or gossip. It might be fun at the time, however, if you're seen to be a gossip or loose with sensitive information it sends a very clear signal that you may not be leadership material."*

- **Niall O'Gorman**, Chief Strategy Officer at **ChannelSight.com**
20 YEARS OF EXPERIENCE

10. Manage your online presence.

What you do on social media is your own business but keep in mind that your Facebook profile, your Instagram, etc. are not just visible to your friends but also to your colleagues and to recruiters. Your managers will not be impressed if they see you posting about how much you hate your job or that you think your boss is an idiot; consider the image you're projecting and think twice before venting your frustration. Likewise you might not want to make those drunken photos public either – whether it's you posting them, or your friends. What you're putting out there today may haunt you forever.

11. Be reliable.

Be that person that people can count on. Meet the deadlines, deliver your projects, be collaborative. You want to be the one that managers choose when they have an important project to assign, the one they recommend for a new position, the one they think of when a promotion comes up.

"Work is not a popularity contest but you might be surprised by how fast someone's reputation for delivering results and supporting a team's overall objectives can travel across an organisation.

A junior manager should bring clarity and focus to problems, make meaningful contributions to the team, always treat people with respect and exude the kind of positive energy that contributes to a productive working environment and high-performance organisation.

At work, as in life, a smile and a kind word also can go a long way towards building a strong management team and a professional reputation."

- Tom O'Brien, Managing Director & Partner at Lovebite, Client Service Director at LOLA Mullen Lowe
32 YEARS OF EXPERIENCE

"Do what you say you're going to do, when you say you're going to do it. Keep the formula simple, under promise and over deliver... always! Build a relationship with your colleagues; find out how you can help them and how they can help you."

- Niall O'Gorman, Chief Strategy Officer at ChannelSight.com
20 YEARS OF EXPERIENCE

12. Just do it.

This is not a buffet where you pick and choose projects based on what you fancy; you have to work on the tasks given to you by your boss, it's as simple as that. There will inevitably be boring tasks like budget tracking, printing copies of presentations, doing your travel expenses, and other tasks that you just don't enjoy. Stop complaining and just get on with it! And, for extra points, why not take the opportunity to see if you can improve even these menial tasks? Maybe others are struggling too – can you create a template? Set up a training session? Streamline or even automate the process? Find ways to add value, even on the little things.

"For me, hard work, dedication and demonstrating that you are a team player focused on results are key. Forget the politics and focus on what your boss needs you to

deliver and deliver it with excellence. There isn't a boss who doesn't appreciate that."

- Michelle Crossan, Vice-President for Strategy & Transformation, Europe
20 YEARS OF EXPERIENCE

"My mantra for a new hire would be 'just do everything' – people discover talents (and things they love) only by doing, hence keep trying new things. When I first started working, I was an engineer and I would never have imagined later working in finance and marketing, writing books, establishing my own company..."

- Vincenzo Carrara, Director, Author, Entrepreneur
15 YEARS OF EXPERIENCE

13. Stay positive and don't get emotional.

Your attitude will be one of your key success drivers – or will block you from progressing. Even in the face of constant changes, last-minute deadlines and never-ending issues, try to stay positive; enjoy the challenge of trying to find a solution! As you'll soon discover, solving issues is a huge part of being a manager, so you'd better get used to it. When emotions are running high, take a deep breath and remember: it's not personal. Go outside for some air, go and cry in the cloakroom if that's what you need to do; then dry your eyes, get on with your work, and reward yourself later with a dinner with friends, a big glass of wine, or a good session at the gym.

"I wish I had known how important your attitude is – being trustworthy, agile, dynamic and enthusiastic, demonstrating leadership skills and being able to formulate ideas and thinking verbally and in writing –

versus anything else at work. Perception is super important in the beginning and it follows you throughout your career; it's difficult to change it later."

- Zsofia Nagy, Brand Manager at Procter & Gamble
9 YEARS OF EXPERIENCE

"Learn quickly that leadership starts with you. To be a leader you must learn that personal leadership is the first step before you can even have a team report to you. This means getting team members excited about the mission or project, helping them when they need it, staying positive in face of adversity and always having the end result in mind."

- Michelle Crossan, Vice-President for Strategy & Transformation, Europe
20 YEARS OF EXPERIENCE

That's it for Chapter 1: Establishing Yourself in the Pack! There are some pretty basic principles in this first chapter, but you'd be surprised how many new managers fail on many of these points. Take the time to review the chapter and think about how you're performing in each area and where you might improve, before moving on to the next chapter.

WOLF TIP: *"Rule 2: Take notes" is our NO-MISS rule in this chapter. It sounds so simple, but it's incredibly powerful both in the impression it gives to management and in allowing you to really own a particular project and its actions.*

We suggest that you review each of the points and think about where you need to focus your attention. To do so, unlock your exclusive access to the free bonus materials, including the worksheet for Chapter 1, on our Wolf Leaders Academy website at: www.wolfleaders.com/FirstJobBonus.

When you're ready, move on to Chapter 2.

CHAPTER 2: UNDERSTANDING THE PACK HIERARCHY

Working with your boss

CHAPTER 2: UNDERSTANDING THE PACK HIERARCHY

Working with your boss

First of all, let's make one thing clear: your boss is your boss for a reason. You may not like her* or her way of doing things but she is your boss, with all the experience, credibility, and allies in the company that come with that position. You can either fight that, or you can accept that she's your boss and try to work with her rather than against her. We suggest working with her given that she's the one who'll determine how your performance is evaluated and what your next assignment will be – and she can make your life hell if she wants to!

To avoid the clumsy "he or she" formulation or the grammatically incorrect singular "they" we've chosen to assume that your boss is a "she" for the purposes of this book. Given decades of inequality in favour of the male sex, we trust that you can forgive our preference in this particular instance...

14. Clarify your working styles.

Your boss will have a preferred way of working and specific expectations on what you should be delivering. It's in your interest to learn what these preferences are, so be sure to ask: how does she prefer to communicate (face to face, chat, email...)? How often (should you send a summary once a week or interrupt her regularly as needed)? How much does she want to be involved (should you keep her informed of every detail or involve her only when you're stuck)? Taking the time to clarify this now will save you a lot of grief later on; and once you know the expectations you can go ahead and exceed them!

"When I arrived, a colleague told me to be clear on my boss's expectations, as it was the key for success. Coming out of university, you're used to doing your best and being your own boss; it doesn't always come naturally to think that what you think is the best might not be the same for someone else."

- Lavinia Desideri, Senior Financial Analyst at Procter & Gamble
8 YEARS OF EXPERIENCE

"A junior manager should try to adapt himself to the rhythm of the organisation and the boss's management style.

If the boss doesn't suggest a forum for regular communication and feedback, it is absolutely correct for the junior employee to propose a process: e.g. a weekly status report, monthly meetings to review progress versus objectives, or regular calls.

With so many different organisational tools available, it is essential that the junior and senior manager get on the same page quickly. No sense in preparing a weekly status report by email if the boss prefers less formal daily updates via Whatsapp or Slack."

- Tom O'Brien, Managing Director & Partner at Lovebite, Client Service Director at LOLA Mullen Lowe
32 YEARS OF EXPERIENCE

15. Help your boss to help you.

Although a good boss will try her very best to understand you, she is not telepathic. Just as you want to understand how she works, you need to tell her what makes you tick. What motivates you? What are your strengths? What are your weaknesses? Where do you need more support? Take control and be clear on how your boss can help you to deliver your best work.

> *"You can't lead others if you can't lead yourself. Therefore, know what you need in order to perform as well as possible and to be happy. Don't be afraid to explain your needs or future ambitions (beyond the existing position) to your manager. Most managers would rather help develop their employees than have them leave the company! In the end, an employment is a bit like a relationship – an open dialogue with mutual respect enables growth."*

- Rita Gustafsson, Head of Sales & Business Development at Bombardier Transportation
9 YEARS OF EXPERIENCE

> *"Relationships with your boss usually take place productively when expectations and deliverables are clearly defined. The 'WHAT' is the critical element to be aligned; the 'HOW' should be in your hands, provided you are enabled to leverage your boss whenever any support is needed in delivering within the aligned frame. If the frame changes over time, make sure to align the changes. If anything goes wrong, speak up."*

- Michel Lambert, Global Director Media Planning & Operations at Procter & Gamble
28 YEARS OF EXPERIENCE

16. Involve your boss.

Even when you think everything's on track and there are no apparent issues, make sure that you involve your manager at the right time. Share your draft presentations with her well ahead of the deadline to give her sufficient time to provide feedback, and to give you sufficient time to make the necessary changes. If your work is perfect (unlikely, but well done you!) then this simply gives you an opportunity to show off to your boss what you're capable of. You may not want to bother her, but she'll be happy to know that everything's going well.

"There is nothing wrong with a new hire asking management to share their experience or give advice. Given that a junior person cannot be expected to have a detailed business background, the best is for them to undergo a thorough analysis of the data (or conduct expert interviews in case data is not available) and based on that formulate their hypothesis, questions and actions."

- Associate Marketing Director at Johnson & Johnson
13 YEARS OF EXPERIENCE

17. Get alignment.

Align your manager on the key messages for any big meeting: agree the objective, what you want her to say and what you will cover. Make sure she's briefed properly and equipped with the information she needs – basically, make her look good! Likewise, when you're working on an important document, or a potentially controversial email, make sure to agree at least on the principle if not the exact text. This will make sure that she's on your side if things get messy later on – give her the chance to have your back!

"Figure out what the boss is measured on and is trying to accomplish. Then align your work with that, and automatically your boss will look good. Giving credit in

public and criticism face to face is also key."

- **Christopher Engman, Founder & Head of Vendemore**
30 YEARS OF EXPERIENCE

18. Flag issues.

Being late on a project is not the end of the world – if you warn your boss ahead of time, that is. If she thinks everything is on track and she only finds out right before the final deadline that something has gone wrong, it will blow up in her face – and yours. A delay on your project might also have broader implications for other projects in the organisation that you may not be aware of. If you inform your boss that you're going to be late, she may be able to help you to move things along, make sure people are supporting you, and if necessary inform senior management of the issue and get an extension of the deadline. Again, let her protect you, and help you release any potential blockages. Admitting that you are having difficulties, and taking responsibility without blaming others, is a sign of maturity and demonstrates that you're willing to hold yourself accountable.

> *"You will impress me if you can approach me with weaknesses and challenges as well as admit mistakes; keep me briefed ahead of time in the event I need to stand up for the team in relation to other stakeholders. Though I expect this of all my employees, I also know that it can be quite scary to do so. However, hiding problems only prevents the opportunity to make improvements."*

- **Rita Gustafsson, Head of Sales and Business Development at Bombardier Transportation**
9 YEARS OF EXPERIENCE

19. Ask for feedback.

Make sure you're getting feedback on how you're doing. If you're not asking for, and open to, constructive criticism, then frankly you're 'uncoachable' and you won't progress in your career. It doesn't matter how good your boss is: if you're not open to learning from her, then she's wasting her time. Ask for general feedback on an on-going basis in your regular meetings, and for specific feedback after a particularly important meeting or presentation. Don't take negative feedback personally, however: feedback (if given correctly) is about your work, your performance, and not an attack on you as an individual.

20. Be kind to your boss.

SPOILER ALERT Your boss is a human being. Did we shock you now? As you work together, always remember this: your boss has feelings too. So when she spends her time coaching you, or when she takes tasks off your plate so that you can focus on the bigger priorities, consider a little "thank you". When she responds carefully and comprehensively to your long email, acknowledge the response and… say thank you! And when she appears particularly stressed or not herself, why not ask if there's something you can do to help? A little kindness and understanding will go a long way.

> *"Never forget that your boss needs you. They can't do everything on their own!"*
>
> **- Ali Al-Shabibi, Senior Software Architect at Open Networking Laboratory**
> **10 YEARS OF EXPERIENCE**

21. Get to know your one-up manager.

Organise a lunch or a coffee with your manager's boss during your first weeks if possible; if they're very senior, you'll need to liaise with their assistant. This is not about going behind your boss's back, which is the last thing you want to do, but simply a case of managing your visibility. You want them to know who you are when it comes to discussing people and possible roles in the future. Come prepared: ask about their vision for the business, or what they think success looks like for you. It's also a good opportunity to talk about the big projects you're working on – just make sure you stick to the big picture and don't go too much into the details (especially the details that your own boss doesn't know about!).

> *"In a new job, you want to spend 33% of your time with other new hires – because they will be your friends for life, your work network no matter where you will be later on. Spend 33% with one level up, because they have made it and you want to know what they have done; they are also the closest to your pains. Lastly you want to spend 33% of your time with two or more levels up, up to the directors and general managers – because these are the people you are seeking as sponsors and mentors in your career."*
>
> **- Luigi Matrone, CEO & Founder of E-Business Institute**
> **10 YEARS OF EXPERIENCE**

And that's Chapter 2: Understanding the Pack Hierarchy. We've moved on from the image you're projecting to how you're working with your boss, someone who'll be critical to how you progress in your career as well as how much you enjoy day-to-day life in the office. Take the time to read through each of the points and think about which areas could do with a bit more focus.

WOLF TIP: *"Rule 19: Ask for feedback" is our NO-MISS rule in this chapter. It requires both courage and humility to ask your boss and your colleagues how you're doing and how you can improve but this really is* *the fastest way in which you can improve your management and leadership skills.*

As in Chapter 1, we suggest that you review the rules in this chapter and identify the ones where you feel you need some extra work. If you haven't already done so, please go to our Wolf Leaders site at <u>www.wolfleaders.com/FirstJobBonus</u> to unlock your exclusive access to the free bonus materials, including the worksheet for Chapter 2.

When you're ready, move on to Chapter 3.

CHAPTER 3: BEING SMART WITH YOUR RESOURCES

Managing your time and energy effectively

CHAPTER 3: BEING SMART WITH YOUR RESOURCES

Managing your time and energy effectively

You may find yourself twiddling your thumbs in the very first days of your new job but soon the projects will be piling up and the emails flooding your inbox, and you'll be struggling to keep your head above water. You won't be able to do everything, and you certainly won't be able to do everything alone. Learning some techniques early on will ensure that you stay focused and on top of your workload – before it's too late....

22. Make choices.

Pay attention now, as this is a big one: make sure you identify which projects will have the biggest impact and then focus your time on those projects. Don't get distracted by all the little tasks and details; instead, take a step back and think about where you're really creating value. Keep your eye on the ball, on what's really important. The simple act of producing PowerPoint presentations and sending long emails does not in itself make you productive. Make sure, of course, that you agree any shift in focus with your manager, to ensure that the priorities you've identified match those of the business.

> *"Don't fall into the typical trap of mistaking activity for result. Whatever the mission, assignment, job – be sure that you know what the desired outcome is in terms of 'how will the company or brand or group benefit from what I'm doing?' There are way too many 'box tickers' around. Don't be one of them."*

- Michel Jouveaux, Founder, Composer & Musician at SoundAdvice, Marketing Consultant at Idea Bakery
20 YEARS OF EXPERIENCE

WOLF TOOL: THE 80-20 PRINCIPLE

The 80-20 or Pareto principle predicts that 20% of the projects will deliver 80% of the value; the remaining 80% of projects will have low or zero output. To stay ahead of the pack you need to identify this 20% - the big projects that will make a difference in your organisation and deliver significant business results – and focus your time and energy on these.

For more on this principle and to download a related exercise to help you to reprioritise your time and energy, visit www.wolfleaders.com/FirstJobBonus to get the full pack of free bonuses.

"It is critical to ensure alignment with your management on what those top projects are, and what is the minimum needed on the rest. You don't want to just choose your own 20% and let the others slide, just to later discover that your management prioritised differently or set the minimum in a different place than you did. Proactive pre-alignment on priorities and success measures can go a long way to focus you on the right 20% and avoid issues."

- Mary Carmen Gasco-Buisson, Global Brand Director at Procter & Gamble
19 YEARS OF EXPERIENCE

23. Make time for the softer skills.

Take a proper lunch break, go to corporate training sessions, join the team drinks – these are all opportunities to learn, to network, to reflect. "I have too much to do" is a foolish and arrogant excuse, which means either that you're not on top of your workload or that you think that your projects are somehow more important than the projects of everyone else who does participate. Missing out on these opportunities will make you less competitive versus your peers who did make the time: think about the bigger picture, the longer term and not just today's little to-do list.

24. Be proactive.

Take the lead on your projects: organise kick-off meetings and share a roadmap with key milestones and deliverables, outline clearly who does what in the team, plan to involve management at the right time, anticipate issues and propose solutions before they develop into full-blown crises. Simply reacting to what gets thrown at you will mean that you're constantly fighting fires and not in control of your workload. You risk being at the mercy of other people's agendas, and at the end of the day you'll need to stay on to do the work that you had actually intended to do. This is especially important on 'long-lead' projects, i.e. projects that cannot be rushed but require input from different people, creative work from agencies, or a fixed block of time for things like product development or testing.

> *"In any corporation that respects new hires and values them for their potential, the biggest mistake a new hire can do is to become a 'yes man' (or woman), waiting for the manager to tell them exactly what to do, wearing blinders from day one and compromising on bringing new ideas to work. Yes men are easily replaceable; so as a manager, if I have to fight to keep someone in my team, who would I fight for? The young new hire who gives me fresh ideas*

and brings his humble contribution to the team – or the one who is just doing his homework? I know my answer."

- **Luigi Matrone, Founder & CEO of E-Business Institute**
11 YEARS OF EXPERIENCE

"In general, junior people in my organisation inspire me with their optimism, their willingness to learn, their desire to make a difference and the opportunity their fresh sets of eyes can bring to existing problems. That's a given.

My colleagues (be they junior managers or seasoned directors) exceed my expectations when they deliver results quicker than expected, under budget and/or with insight and analysis beyond what was originally requested.

To truly impress me, however, a member of my team should perform all of the above and also anticipate the organisation's needs by proactively solving a problem, seizing an opportunity to improve results or the organisation and/or providing a novel, inventive or creative approach to a business issue."

- **Tom O'Brien, Managing Director & Partner at Lovebite, Client Service Director at LOLA Mullen Lowe**
32 YEARS OF EXPERIENCE

WOLF TOOL: THE URGENT-IMPORTANT MATRIX

This time management matrix is a tool created by Stephen Covey, author of *The 7 Habits of Highly Effective People*, based on the principle that daily tasks can be organised into four different categories according to (i) how urgent the task is and (ii) how important it is. The goal is to change the way you're working so that you're spending most of your time in the top right 'important but not urgent' quadrant. Working on important tasks before they become urgent will ensure that you are giving the big priorities the time they deserve while avoiding 'fire fighting' due to lack of planning or having wasted time on less important tasks.

For more on this matrix and to download a related exercise to help you to better organise your time, visit www.wolfleaders.com/FirstJobBonus to get the full pack of free bonuses.

"Make sure you focus your time on your projects and not on 'stuff' that insidiously creeps up on you. We live in an age of information overload and you need to be even better at filtering and focusing if you're to actually accomplish anything."

- Pauline Manos, Independent Consultant, Trainer & Mentor 24 YEARS OF EXPERIENCE

"I really suggest that you focus relentlessly on your top 3 – max top 5 – priorities. Organise your deliverables around those priorities. If they do not relate, park them for your spare time; you may realise that those are not really needed. Start every day, every week, reorganising your deliverables in terms of importance and urgency."

- Michel Lambert, Global Director Media Planning & Operations at Procter & Gamble 28 YEARS OF EXPERIENCE

25. Ask questions.

You're not expected to know everything from day one so take the opportunity to ask, and to learn. Think of this as your apprenticeship period! People soon forget what it was like to be a new hire and they won't necessarily recognise the need to explain things unless you speak up. It's better to ask 'stupid' questions at the beginning than to pretend that you know everything and then mess up further down the line. Most people are more than willing to help.

"Always ask if you are not sure of something. It is easier to get advice and do things right the first time than doing things wrong and spending time fixing them."

**- Outi Virtanen, Brand Manager at Nordic Cosmetics
14 YEARS OF EXPERIENCE**

"Asking questions, especially as a new hire in a new role, is GOOD – not asking and trying to solve everything on your own is not always the best approach. Trying to get feedback and insights from people who have been around for a while is smart and definitely doesn't make you look stupid."

**- Aliki Anagnostopoulos, Consumer & Market Knowledge Manager at Procter & Gamble
8 YEARS OF EXPERIENCE**

"The biggest mistake I have seen a new hire make is to give solutions (or, worse yet, commands) before fully understanding the challenge. I have seen new hires let their ambitions get the best of them and give some silly, uninformed points of view in the desire to appear assertive and in-control. While today's business environment needs agility and 'real time' decision-making, it still requires

sound judgement. Ask questions. Listen – then make decisions."

- Tom O'Brien, Managing Director & Partner at Lovebite, Client Service Director at LOLA Mullen Lowe
32 YEARS OF EXPERIENCE

26. Ask for support.

We said you need to work hard, yes, but you shouldn't be killing yourself under an unreasonable workload. If you're feeling overwhelmed, make sure you check in with your boss's expectations so that you don't stay late working on a 50-page presentation when all she wanted was a short email. Is someone in the team not pulling his weight? Your boss can help you to make sure you have the resources you need. Struggling to find the data you need? Someone in your team may have access to the data, or be able to work with you to make some reasonable assumptions. Having trouble with your boss? Find a trusted mentor with whom you can discuss the best approach. Don't suffer in silence.

"You should not buckle under the pressure when it comes to situations where you have to do the harder right versus the easier wrong. This is especially difficult for a junior person, since they might think that they do not have the right experience to judge the specific situation, or in other cases, they might be fooled into an unethical situation. In such cases, I suggest that they listen to their gut and reach out to someone they trust who has high moral standards."

- Bora Karamustafa, Independent Consultant in Marketing, Sales & Supply Chain Management
18 YEARS OF EXPERIENCE

27. Leverage your strengths.

You will do your best work, and hence make the biggest contribution to the business, if you make the most of your strengths. No one can be good at absolutely everything, so recognise your weaknesses and find ways to compensate, for example by collaborating with people whose strengths complement yours. There are some skills that we all need to learn – clear business writing, basic presentation skills, time management, and so on – but beyond that, the real magic happens where your skills and passions intersect with the nature of the projects you're working on. If you love team building, share with your boss your ideas about bringing this to the organisation. If you're a numbers beast, why not apply your thinking to an area of the business that's lacking robust data analysis?

"Absorb the culture of the place and see how you can reconcile what is expected of you with what you know to be your core strengths. If you don't know precisely what these are, which wouldn't be a surprise as one tends to only ask oneself those questions later in a career, find a mentor who can help you articulate them within the first six months on the job. The best relationships happen when you're given the opportunity to play to your strengths in a way that whatever company you're in really needs."

- **Michel Jouveaux, Founder, Composer & Musician at SoundAdvice, Marketing Consultant at Idea Bakery**
20 YEARS OF EXPERIENCE

"Identify where your personal strengths and the most important needs of your company or business intersect, and focus your work in those areas. While the first years of your career will be learning oriented (as they should be), working on important business needs from the beginning will accelerate your level of influence and

contribution to the company, and working in things that leverage your natural strengths will give you the self-confidence and energy that stems from early wins. Both will also give you visibility and help build a critical support network that will ensure a virtuous cycle of getting great assignments, learning more and faster, delivering more results, which then leads to more important assignment, etc."

- **Mary Carmen Gasco-Buisson, Global Brand Director at Procter & Gamble**
19 YEARS OF EXPERIENCE

28. Don't reinvent the wheel.

Excellent work is not always original work: there are plenty of lessons to be extracted from previous initiatives, from other categories, from other regions. Don't hesitate to re-apply these insights – you'll be standing on the shoulders of giants and you'll be able to deliver results much faster when you don't have to create everything from scratch.

"I always say 'copy with pride', meaning that if you see something that is done really well (maybe by a competitor) then make your own version of it to drive success.

Also, 'mi casa es su casa', meaning share your good ideas and what you have done successfully with others in order to cultivate a positive business environment."

- **Outi Virtanen, Brand Manager at Nordic Cosmetics**
14 YEARS OF EXPERIENCE

29. Learn to push back.

It's very rare that a task is really THAT urgent – and even if it is, that doesn't mean that it's necessarily important. *[See the "Urgent-Important Matrix", page 44.]* Often it's simply the result of someone else not having planned properly – if that's the case then push back, politely, and ask for a more reasonable deadline. Two exceptions here: first, if it's your boss or a more senior manager then you should go ahead and deliver, unless you absolutely believe that you have something much more urgent and important that takes precedence, in which case you should ask your boss if this new request supersedes the old one; and second if you do, in fact, have time to deliver the work then it's nice to help out a colleague in need, and helping them now will also mean that you'll be able to call in a favour next time when you're the one who's in trouble.

> *"I wish I had known what 'less is more' means and how you can actually shine by saying no, shutting something down instead of adding something new.*
>
> *A few months after I started, I received a very exciting extra project and got a lot of freedom to take the project in different directions. Although it was non-essential, I continued to drive it further despite multiple obstacles. The more we were invested, the more difficult it was to see the obvious: this project was too complex.*
>
> *It took six months of work before I considered recommending shutting it down and not replacing it with anything else. I wrote a proper recommendation to make sure we would not redo the same mistake a few months later, and not only was this easily aligned with top management but this was also seen as a real stepping up of my leadership behaviour."*

- **Mathias Avramov, Assistant Brand Manager at Procter & Gamble**
5 YEARS OF EXPERIENCE

Congratulations, you've completed Chapter 3: Being Smart With Your Resources and made it halfway through the book! How are you in this area? What do you think you should focus on? Review each of the points before moving on to the next chapter.

WOLF TIP: *"Rule 22: Make choices" is our NO-MISS rule in this chapter. The more you progress in your career, the more this rule will help you in carving out time for what matters the most.*

Make sure that you review the rules in this chapter and start practising the ones where you feel you could really improve. Don't forget that you can visit our Wolf Leaders Academy website at <u>www.wolfleaders.com/FirstJobBonus</u> to unlock your exclusive access to the free bonus materials, including the worksheet for Chapter 3 as well as the exercises to go with the 80-20 Principle and the Urgent-Important Matrix.

When you're ready, move on to Chapter 4.

CHAPTER 4: SHARPENING YOUR INSTINCTS

Developing your thinking in the face of uncertainty

CHAPTER 4: SHARPENING YOUR INSTINCTS

Developing your thinking in the face of uncertainty

You may be new but your very newness means that you are in the perfect position to bring a fresh perspective on the business. Even as a junior manager, you're perfectly capable of bringing your own thoughts and insights to your work; in fact, you're expected to do so. Doing some independent analysis and showing management that you're thinking for yourself is hugely important in demonstrating your leadership potential.

30. Have an opinion.

When you're asked a question, the one answer that is completely unsatisfactory is "I don't know." You should always be able to formulate some kind of opinion, even if based on assumptions or first impressions. If it's a question requiring data that you don't have, just be honest and admit that you don't know the answer right now but "I'll find out." This shows that you're self-aware and confident enough to admit the limits of your knowledge but prepared to do the extra work to correct this.

> *"The most powerful tip I ever received was that just because you're an entry-level manager doesn't mean you should think like one. Being creative, taking ownership of the business and looking at the big, strategic picture is your responsibility as well. Your learning curve will be far steeper than your peers who never really look beyond their day-to-day tasks. And your managers will notice (and appreciate) it."*

- Sam Murphy, Assistant Brand Manager at Procter & Gamble
3 YEARS OF EXPERIENCE

"Always voice your opinion. Don't ask for permission to speak; don't be shy. You'll only hinder your own career! There is no point in having ideas if no one hears them.

Stand up to your boss and challenge them: just because they are the boss doesn't mean that they know more than you do."

- Ali Al-Shabibi, Senior Software Architect at Open Networking Laboratory
10 YEARS OF EXPERIENCE

"The project manager is in the best possible position to make decisions as he is at the centre of the discussions, receiving input from all stakeholders, hearing all sides of the same issue, being 'in the know' – as such, not being able to have at least an educated opinion on the topic with this wealth of information translates into laziness or lack of courage. Great project managers systematically ask themselves the question: What do I think? What would I do here? What does the information tell me? What do I think is the right answer?

People are employed to think, to add value, to make choices. Otherwise, project management software such as Microsoft Project would be used to deal with this – a scary thought."

- Kenny Kerswell, Senior Consultant at Kinetic Consulting
15 YEARS OF EXPERIENCE

31. Keep asking, "why?"

When faced with a problem, call on your inner child and keep asking WHY until you get to the root of an issue. Try asking "why?" five times: Why do you have this result? Why did that happen? Why was that the case? Why? Why?! Don't be satisfied with a superficial explanation that may only touch on the symptoms rather than the fundamental cause.

> *"I think the most important tip is to use your brain and not to be afraid – it's easy to fall into the trap of doing the small and easy tasks versus the big things that matter the most."*

- Zsofia Nagy, Brand Manager at Procter & Gamble
9 YEARS OF EXPERIENCE

32. Get comfortable with uncertainty.

Hypotheses, estimations and assumptions are your friends when you don't have the complete knowledge or data and you need to act fast. You're never going to have all the answers, so you need to find ways to cope without all that information. Are there case studies you can look into to give you an indication of what is a reasonable benchmark? Can you do some ballpark calculations? Outline a few different possibilities and then discuss it with your manager? There is always some information you can use to make an educated guess.

> *"A good manager is a person capable of making choices and sticking to them unless new information or altered dynamics require a change. Lack of decision making, continual changes in decisions or conversely no change even when the landscape changes are the most detrimental factors for managing a business. Obviously it is about making the 'right' choices but sometimes we don't have all the answers so go with what your gut tells you and adjust*

as you get more information; just don't leave the organisation in limbo."

- Vincenzo Carrara, Director, Author, Entrepreneur
15 YEARS OF EXPERIENCE

"My number 1 tip to a new hire is to **TAKE RISKS.** *'It is better to do and beg forgiveness than ask permission.' Too many people are far too timid and afraid to make things happen. They fail to impress their management and get branded quickly as 'low impact' people. Businesses need people who push the envelope, take risks, make things happen. This is particularly crucial in today's fast-changing world. Our 'personal branding' starts from day one in a job and once a person has a given brand equity it is damn hard to change it."*

- James Lafferty, **CEO** of British American Tobacco Philippines
30 YEARS OF EXPERIENCE

33. Don't bring problems, bring solutions.

When requesting help from your boss or from a colleague, be sure to still prepare different scenarios or solutions ahead of time to serve as a basis for the discussion and to show that you've thought it through. As a new hire, you will be bringing fresh ideas and new ways of looking at things and it's important to get this input before you're influenced by the prevailing wisdom! This does not mean, however, that you should be afraid to talk openly about problems or to ask questions when needed.

"In terms of solutions, I would not wait to have 'the right answer' before coming to management, but always at least have a rough outline of potential options to explore as to

how to solve the problem, how you plan to evaluate them, what help you need, and your anticipated timing. This will (i) help to make sure that you really understand the issue, (ii) give an actionable structure to the discussion (versus a chaotic problem-sharing session with no clear action plan coming out of it), and (iii) show your leadership, maturity, and ability to manage issues like this."

- Mary Carmen Gasco-Buisson, Global Brand Director at Procter & Gamble
19 YEARS OF EXPERIENCE

"New hires bring fresh ideas, new ways of looking at things, and they should feel comfortable in bringing solutions and suggestions to management... but this shouldn't be interpreted as being afraid to talk openly about problems or not feeling welcome to ask questions, as often happens, much to the disadvantage of all involved. We need very open lines of communication these days."

- Pauline Manos, Independent Consultant, Trainer & Mentor
24 YEARS OF EXPERIENCE

34. Make choices (yes, again!).

When making your recommendations, don't just give a laundry list of different options. Make *choices*. What is the most likely scenario out of the possibilities? What is your one recommended course of action? You need to be making choices whether it's a question of key messages in a long presentation, making strategic decisions, or identifying top priorities for your work plan. Resources are always limited – time, people, money – so you have to focus the organisation on what really matters.

"Strategy is choice. Not choosing is not a strategy. Shoot broad, fail bad. Sounds pedantic but remains true."

- **Michel Jouveaux, Founder, Composer & Musician at SoundAdvice, Marketing Consultant at Idea Bakery**
20 YEARS OF EXPERIENCE

WOLF TOOL: THE RULE OF THREE

People remember things more easily when they come in a triad: just think of *Liberté, Egalité, Fraternité*; *Sex, Drugs and Rock'n'roll*; *Veni, Vidi, Vici*... This applies in business as well, and you will encounter it often.

Following the rule of three will force you to make choices. It will demonstrate to management that you are not just providing a long shopping list of possible drivers, scenarios, or actions but you've done the work and have identified the three that are the most important.

---

35. Be flexible and learn from your mistakes.

There is no weakness in changing your opinion if you get new data or insights after thinking about it for longer or after talking it through with your boss or colleagues. It's much better to recognise this early on and to redirect your course than to keep going down the wrong path. Mistakes are learning opportunities. The company culture may be more or less risk averse, but at this stage of your career you can absolutely afford to make mistakes as long as you recognise them as mistakes and learn from them, making sure that you don't make the same one again.

"My number one tip to a new hire is to strive to learn from both success and failure. Stay humble in the knowledge

that you will never know everything... and take the time to connect and listen."

- **Tania Zwicky, Associate Director, Procter & Gamble**
19 YEARS OF EXPERIENCE

"I have seen many passionate new hires become deflated when they perceive their ideas are not being heard by the more experienced folk in their teams. Take every rejection as a chance to refine your selling approach and to improve your idea."

- **Michelle Crossan, Vice-President for Strategy & Transformation, Europe**
20 YEARS OF EXPERIENCE

36. Keep It Simple, Stupid (KISS).

Often the simplest solutions are the best – don't think you'll look smart by making things unnecessarily complex! A leader who really understands what they're doing can give a succinct presentation, get their message across in a short email or summarise the key points in a brief document. As Mark Twain once said, "I didn't have time to write a short letter, so I wrote a long one instead." Take the time to write the short letter!

"Think: kitchen logic. If your mother cannot understand what you are talking about then the likelihood is that your consumer won't understand it either!"

- **Associate Marketing Director at Johnson & Johnson**
13 YEARS OF EXPERIENCE

In Chapter 4: Sharpening your Instincts, we've started to get a bit more technical about applying your analytical thinking in a business context. As before, make sure that you review all the points and choose the ones you want to focus on, before moving on to the next chapter. It's so easy to skim through these paragraphs but you'll only develop your leadership skills by actually applying them to real situations or problems at work.

WOLF TIP: *"Rule 36: Keep It Simple, Stupid" is our NO-MISS rule in this chapter. If you are unable to explain your idea in a few sentences, then it's just not clear enough.*

The worksheet for Chapter 4 is available to help you review the most important rules for your own personal development, along with the rest of the bonus materials, on our Wolf Leaders website at: www.wolfleaders.com/FirstJobBonus.

When you're ready, move on to Chapter 5.

CHAPTER 5: COMMUNICATING WITH THE PACK

Getting your message across effectively

CHAPTER 5: COMMUNICATING WITH THE PACK

Getting your message across effectively

Managing emails, calls and meetings effectively will be critical to staying on top of your projects as well as how you are perceived by the broader organisation. You've grown up with computers and iPhones and email and chat and you're completely comfortable navigating this world – but that's not necessarily the case for the older generations of managers in the company, and you need to be sensitive to this fact. Business communication also requires a different style and professionalism than Snapchatting with your friends, just in case you're wondering.

37. Don't let email dictate your agenda.

As both your inbox and your agenda begin to fill up, you'll struggle to keep up with the constant stream of emails; trying to do so will allow your inbox to dictate your agenda and you will no longer be in control. Schedule time to review your email in the morning and again after lunch, then maybe one more time in the late afternoon – these two or three slots a day will make sure you're identifying any burning issues or requests. Make sure you communicate this approach to your boss and to your team and give them a back-up: tell them that you'll be reachable on the phone or on chat in case of emergency. Consider also creating a rule so that emails from particular senders like your boss are highlighted in a bright colour so that you see them and action them right away.

"Always start your working day with what is important. This may be likely an important project rather than the last emails. Once you have progressed with the important tasks, as defined by your to-do list, then you can handle urgent matters. If an email requires more than a few

minutes to handle, transform it into a specific task to be categorised in your to-do list. Prioritise your tasks in function of the deadlines and workload that is required."

- **Michel Lambert, Global Director Media Planning & Operations at Procter & Gamble**
28 YEARS OF EXPERIENCE

WOLF TOOL:
DO IT – DEFER IT – DELEGATE IT

When you're going through your emails, you want to do so as efficiently as possible. This means minimising the number of times you have to open and read each email, taking valuable time away from doing actual work. Choose which of the following three actions to apply to each email:

1. Do it now
2. Defer it
3. Delegate it

For more on these three different actions and to download a related exercise to help you to manage your email inbox, visit www.wolfleaders.com/FirstJobBonus to get the full pack of bonuses.

---

38. Make effective use of email.

Email was never intended to be used as a real-time communication medium, nor for long and complex discussions. It does, however, have an important role to play when asking or answering a simple question, informing a large group of people on a simple topic, or communicating on something where having a written message track is important. In these instances, make sure that you use an explicit subject line e.g. "for information" or "action required" to clarify the action that you're expecting; don't send an essay expecting the recipient to read from start to finish; don't send 20MB files that will clutter up their inboxes; send group emails only when absolutely necessary; and avoid that "reply all" button that drives everyone mad. Think: what would happen if everyone sent an email like this?

> *"Email communication has become vital in today's business life because this is one of the very few effective communication vehicles to reach all stakeholders. However, the attention that we get from an email does not exceed five or ten seconds. In those very few seconds, we must identify the topic, the expected action and the rationale. If those do not come out clearly, it will likely result in misinterpretation or missed deliverables."*
>
> - **Michel Lambert, Global Director Media Planning & Operations at Procter & Gamble**
> **28 YEARS OF EXPERIENCE**

39. After two rounds of emails, pick up the phone.

Speaking of driving everyone mad, if you find that you have to go back and forth on email a couple of times then you should stop and pick up the phone or arrange a short meeting. That way, you can have a quick chat to resolve any question marks and concerns and get to a faster resolution than continuing with endless written discussions. Modern communication tools notwithstanding, good old-fashioned conversation is still important and can be pretty powerful in getting things moving when you're stuck!

40. Be careful using email on sensitive topics.

Emails can be misunderstood, since you're unable to accurately convey a tone or a context, and sensitive or complex issues are usually best handled in person. Face to face is also more effective when you need to ask for help, especially if it's urgent – people are more likely to empathise and will be more willing to help if you're able to put your case to them in person; email is easier to ignore! This is particularly important when you're working in an international environment, as idiom and humour can often be misread when we're dealing with different languages and cultures.

41. Respect people's time.

Before you send out an invite for a two-hour meeting, ask yourself: Is it really necessary? Who needs to be there? How long do you need? What is the objective and what outcome are you looking for? Be clear in the invite if the meeting is "for information only" or "decision needed". Consider a short 'stand-up' meeting if you just need to bring people together for a quick chat. Is there some pre-reading that you can send ahead of time to focus the discussion more effectively during the actual meeting? A bit of preparation in ensuring that you have the right people at the right time focusing on the right objective will save you and everyone involved a lot of time and energy.

> *"I have become a big fan of the following slogan: GEPO – it stands for 'Good Enough, Press On'. A great tool that can be used in a team setting to call out when too much time is being spent on a topic or a discussion."*
>
> **- Kenny Kerswell, Senior Consultant at Kinetic Consulting**
> **15 YEARS OF EXPERIENCE**

42. Own your meetings.

When you start the meeting itself, begin with the objective: tell the audience why you are here. Don't assume that everyone is on the same page, as each attendee might have different expectations. Once everyone is clear on the desired outcome, then you can focus the discussion on achieving that objective. If the discussion veers off topic, suggest politely that you "take the conversation offline" i.e. into a separate meeting and bring the focus back to your meeting's objective. End the meeting with a recap of the key decisions and the next steps, and send a written summary within 24 hours.

> *"Junior people impress me in presentations when they demonstrate enough knowledge to convince the audience, enough confidence to engage the audience, and enough consideration for their audience to give them what they need AND not put them to sleep. The presentation should be focused on influencing the audience... NOT showing off how smart they are."*
>
> **- Tania Zwicky, Associate Director at Procter & Gamble**
> **19 YEARS OF EXPERIENCE**

43. Learn the art of business writing.

Learning to write an effective business document will stand you in good stead for the rest of your career. You'll be able to notify people quickly of developments with a clear overview of the key information, influence them by presenting the data in a conclusive way, and show off the great results of your team with convincing results. Be clear on the objective of the document: are you asking for approval of a recommendation or are you simply sharing information? Don't try to sound clever, instead use clear and concise language and use the active tense rather than passive ("The brand team made the decision..." rather than "The decision was made..."). Remember **"the rule of three"** (page 60). Read and re-read, making sure that there are no typos, which only serve to distract from the content of the document.

"The ability of employees to process complex data, share their thinking in a crisp and clear manner, and drive decisive action is an art that few master.

Regardless of the vehicle (one-page recommendation, issue sheet, PowerPoint presentation, etc.), being able to condense complex issues and thoughts into clear and decisive thinking is a critical skill to possess in any field. The good news is that a substantial portion of this can be trained; more can be acquired via practice."

- Kenny Kerswell, Senior Consultant at Kinetic Consulting
15 YEARS OF EXPERIENCE

WOLF TOOL: WRITING A BUSINESS RECOMMENDATION

The most common document you'll ever write is the business recommendation: a proposal to management requesting approval for a particular course of action. In fact this doesn't have to be a document but can also be an email.

Keep it to one page (that's why we call it a 'one-pager'!), shorter if an email, and use this format as a guide:

1. Opening paragraph
Start by clarifying the objective of the document or email, e.g. This is to get your approval for new initiative X.

2. Background
Summarise any historical information the reader needs to know in order to understand the context for the decision; stick to facts and keep it brief.

3. Recommendation
This is the heart of the document: What is your recommendation? How do you recommend going about

this?

4. Basis for recommendation

Here you provide the rationale: give three reasons for why you are recommending this course of action (any more will confuse and dilute the message). Consider: How will this action improve or resolve the situation? Is there some precedent or case study that you can refer to? What is the data from which you have drawn your conclusions?

5. Indicated Actions

What are the next steps? Specify the action needed, who owns the action, and what is the deadline for completing it.

Make sure you date and 'sign' the document with your name for reference.

"'Ce qui se conçoit bien s'énonce clairement.'" I.e. 'If you can think it clearly – you can write it clearly.' A French 17th-century poet said that and he was right.

There is a fantastic element of strategic thinking discipline at the heart of writing a one-page memo or recommendation. The format forces you to make brutal choices and polish your logic to its utmost level of perfection. In addition to which, it's also a great exercise in marketing – after a while you know your management enough to write them into sawing the board they are sitting on."

- **Michel Jouveaux, Founder, Composer & Musician at SoundAdvice, Marketing Consultant at Idea Bakery**
20 YEARS OF EXPERIENCE

44. Think before you press send.

When it comes to written communication, remember that it can reach an audience and live on far beyond what was originally intended. Don't just forward on long email chains – or, if you do, make sure you check what's in there, as you don't want a senior director to read your banter about the weekend. In all your written communication, try to imagine: What if this were printed on the front page of *The Times* or on the desk of the CEO? This can help you to keep it professional and appropriate for any audience.

> *"Apply the 'New York Times rule' for any written communication. Emails, memos and other documents always end up travelling in unexpected ways, for good or for bad. By ensuring that you treat each piece of content as if it were going to be printed on the first page of a famous newspaper and seen by everyone including top management and your family, you naturally make better decisions about what you're writing and how you're conveying your message.*
>
> *This has another side effect, which is that you can be proud and feel happy about what you produce, send and share, instead of feeling robot fatigue after the X emails you send every day and the Y documents you prepare each week."*
>
> **- Mathias Avramov, Assistant Brand Manager at Procter & Gamble**
> **5 YEARS OF EXPERIENCE**

Almost there! In Chapter 5: Communicating with the Pack we've started to look out into the broader organisation and consider how you can get your message across effectively, whether you're sending an email to an individual or presenting to a whole room of people. Think of where you want to focus your attention and then, when you're ready, move on to the final chapter.

WOLF TIP: *"Rule 43: Learn the art of business writing" is our NO-MISS rule in this chapter. This is hard and will require commitment from you along with coaching from your manager and colleagues, but it will make a huge difference in your career.*

Refer to the worksheet for Chapter 5 in order to anchor your learning, available along with the rest of the bonus materials at www.wolfleaders.com/FirstJobBonus.

When you're ready, move on to Chapter 6.

CHAPTER 6: LOOKING AFTER THE PACK

Engaging the multi-functional team

CHAPTER 6: LOOKING AFTER THE PACK

Engaging the multi-functional team

You can't be a leader without people to lead; as such, your team will be critical to your success. You need to understand the people you're working with, get them on board with your vision, energise and excite them... and, above all, you need to get on with them! These are the people you're going to be working with in the coming months and years and you want to be having fun together; otherwise you'll never enjoy your job, however meaningful you find the work itself.

45. Get to know your team.

Meet with the new members of your team to understand the scope of each of their roles, their background, their style of working and their current priorities. You're bound to meet somebody you don't like or don't immediately get on with but however difficult it is on a professional or a personal level, you're going to have to not only work with them but do all you can to get the best out of them. A good place to start is with the assumption that everybody wants to do a good job.

> *"The best advice I got when I started was to go and talk to everyone! Get to know people to understand the business and your job from different perspectives, from top management to the multifunctional team."*

> - Agathe Marionneau, Brand Manager at Procter & Gamble
> **5 YEARS OF EXPERIENCE**

> *"Make sure that you meet everyone in the wider team and figure out what are their top three tips to add value. Try to*

understand the team culture as soon as you can, always be collaborative, and look for ways to add value to areas outside of your own core scope."

- Dimitris Papalexopoulos, Head of EMEA Sales Development at Google
9 YEARS OF EXPERIENCE

WOLF TOOL: MYERS BRIGGS

Myers Briggs is a personality profiling method that divides the population into 16 personality types. The types are defined by a combination of four letters that summarise the psychological preferences as to how people perceive the world and make decisions. (Some online tests will even allocate you a Star Wars character or an animal, if you want to get a bit more creative!)

Knowing your own profile will allow you to better understand your own behaviour, how you approach challenges and how you interact with people. Knowing the profile of your boss and colleagues will allow you to understand their behaviour and how you can adapt your style and message to better engage with and influence them.

For more on this system and to find out which is your profile, visit www.wolfleaders.com/FirstJobBonus to get the full pack of bonuses including a worksheet for Myers Briggs.

---

46. Understand the larger context.

Understanding the bigger picture will help you to frame your projects in a relevant way to get other people on board. If you know where your project fits within their priorities, you're much more likely to be able to influence them and get them to contribute to your agenda. So try to understand what's making it hard for them to deliver what you're asking of them.

"The failsafe way to get the best out of people at work and in life is to consciously try to really 'see' them. Listen to their point of view and show that you care. Don't assume they share your way of thinking or belief system (or that they should do so). Don't judge them if they don't react the way you expect. Try to understand the person and their circumstances and you'll be amazed how much richer your life will be, and how deep your connection can unexpectedly become."

- Tania Zwicky, Associate Director at Procter & Gamble
19 YEARS OF MANAGEMENT EXPERIENCE

"Network and work across the organisation. In large corporate organisations, the tasks are distributed across a very large number of stakeholders – not necessarily located in the same place. Knowing those stakeholders and understanding their scope of work and priorities will help you to better leverage those resources in a productive way. Do not rely on virtual only; take the time to meet and call. You will then gain respect and support."

- Michel Lambert, Global Director Media Planning & Operations at Procter & Gamble
28 YEARS OF MANAGEMENT EXPERIENCE

47. Be reasonable with your deadlines.

Give other people time to do quality work and keep in mind that your top priority project is not necessarily theirs. A deadline of "tomorrow" or worse still "today" can only ever be the exception, requiring proper justification and, most likely, some powerful persuasive skills. Refer back to the **"Urgent-Important Matrix"**, page 44: just as you don't want people coming to you with urgent requests that are not really important for you, so too you need to avoid doing the same to other people. A special note on agencies and creative teams: creativity especially takes time, so here there is no such thing as tomorrow. More time means better ideas, which will save you time and give you better results in the long run.

> *"I would always introduce myself to people in other functions, especially technical people, by spending time with them and admiring what they do, being curious about their work while admitting I had no clue and needed their help, not forgetting the personal touch of being genuinely interested in what kind of person they are. Only with this personal relationship have I always succeeded, for example, in having last-minute changes that would otherwise not have been accepted, to get that extra piece of work outside office hours, and so on.*
>
> *And don't forget to always let people know what great work they are doing!"*

- Associate Marketing Director at Johnson & Johnson
13 YEARS OF EXPERIENCE

48. Trust that 1 + 1 = 3.

Yes, it sounds cheesy and a bit bohemian but the fact is that we all have different skills and experience to bring to the table. If we come to a negotiation with the immovable belief that we are right and everyone else is wrong, we will miss out on a huge opportunity to learn and get to something that's even better. On the other hand, if we're open to listening to the other person and understand that there might be a third option that is not a compromise but rather a win-win solution, more powerful than what either of us could have imagined going into the discussion, then we are much more likely to reach an agreement that everyone is happy with and that will deliver the results that we are looking for.

> *"In cases where a different skill set, style or function drives a very different focus or approach, I will try to understand where they are coming from, what success looks like for them, and where we can find common goals and interests. The idea is to find ways in which we both can get our needs met, and both grow from our collaboration, while working towards a common purpose."*

- Mary Carmen Gasco-Buisson, Global Brand Director at Procter & Gamble
18 YEARS OF EXPERIENCE

> *"You have to genuinely, and I mean truly genuinely, believe in their value, even though they are different than you and you may have had to struggle to understand that value (because, after all, that value is different than yours, so not so immediately evident). Only then, and only when you truly respect them, can you understand how to leverage them in a team, how to work best with them as an individual, how to make them feel comfortable working with you, different as you are."*

- Pauline Manos, Independent Consultant, Trainer & Mentor
24 YEARS OF EXPERIENCE

49. Give credit where credit is due.

You will shine through the success of your team as a whole.

Management is smart enough to know that big projects are not carried out alone but require a strong team, which in turn requires a strong leader. Do not hesitate to praise your team publicly – far from taking the glory away from your own work, demonstrating the maturity to praise and thank your team is a valued characteristic of a leader and will only strengthen your image, not weaken it.

> *"You're in a team. Be a team player. Or get out."*
>
> - **Michel Jouveaux, Founder, Composer & Musician at SoundAdvice, Marketing Consultant at Idea Bakery**
> **20 YEARS OF EXPERIENCE**

50. Be kind.

Basic human kindness can be the first thing to go in the face of intense pressure and deadlines but this would be a mistake. Business is ultimately about people; so be respectful towards each and every individual, say good morning and goodbye, say thank you and please, ask how someone is doing when they are off sick, bring them a muffin on their birthday... basically, be a human being! Show that you care about the people behind the business, from your director down to the team assistant.

> *"Bring out the best in people by respecting them, thanking them and giving positive feedback for good work. Make them feel that you respect them as individuals and as professionals, cultivate their best features by trusting them; never micromanage them.*
>
> *Even if you need to give negative feedback, do it in a constructive and positive way, because fear and lack of respect kills productivity and leads to bad business decisions."*

**- Outi Virtanen, Brand Manager at Nordic Cosmetics
14 YEARS OF EXPERIENCE**

And that's it, Chapter 6 done and dusted. Well, not quite: as ever, we suggest that you review each of the points and think about where you need to focus your attention. It's when it comes to engaging the multi-functional team that your leadership will become absolutely critical, so take your time with this chapter, re-read the points and think about specific people and situations that can benefit from applying some of these principles.

WOLF TIP: *"Rule 45: Get to know your team" is our NO-MISS rule in this chapter. It's so important for you to get to know your colleagues, both in terms of their roles and in terms of who they are as a person, in order to get your job done – but also so that you have fun and actually enjoy your time in the office!*

You can get the final worksheet for Chapter 6 on our website, at <u>www.wolfleaders.com/FirstJobBonus</u>.

When you're ready... that's it, you've completed the book! Congratulations! Of course, this is only the beginning. We've given you a lot to chew on, so give yourself time to reflect and really think about how you can implement these techniques in your day-to-day working life. We also recommend that you come back to this book in three months' time and review where you are.

Read on for some final thoughts and additional resources.

FINAL THOUGHTS

So how are you feeling? Overwhelmed by all the tips and advice? Feeling confident? Inspired and ready to take on the corporate world? Whatever the case, we've given you plenty to think about in this book and we wish you the best of luck as you start applying these techniques in your day-to-day working life. By choosing to implement even a few of the techniques, you will see great results as you leap well ahead of your peers.

That being said, this is not about getting ahead at any cost, elbowing other people out of the way as you chop your way to the top. This is about being the best that you can be, learning techniques that will enhance and enable your natural strengths and talents. We want you to develop into a strong, well-respected leader who is creating real value with work that you can be proud of.

Becoming a true alpha leader means not just working effectively and efficiently but also looking at the bigger picture of how you want to define success in your own life. As we gathered insights from across our network, this point came through loud and clear: life's too short to spend your life in a job that you hate, so you need to do everything you can to create a job, and a career, that will give you both meaning and joy for years to come. With this in mind, we leave you with some of these nuggets from our most experienced managers…

"You only live once: make it count! While many people apply this to life outside of work, I also apply it to work. I want to make a positive, meaningful and substantial difference, no matter what role I am in – and I want to do it in a way that will leave me fulfilled and happy with myself when it's all over."

- **Mary Carmen Gasco-Buisson, Global Brand Director at Procter & Gamble**

"Your professional reputation is like a bonsai tree, needing constant care and attention over a long period of time. While a wrong move can be damaging and take time to recover from its rarely fatal. So long as you learn from the experience you may have gained some wisdom. Have fun!"

- Niall O'Gorman, Chief Strategy Officer at ChannelSight.com

"Ask yourself WHY you are doing the job you are doing. Is this the real place where you want to be? Is it fulfilling your passion and purpose? Are you happy to work with the type of people you have around right now? We are a generation that will deny the 'job for life' type of culture. There is incredible value to be taken from any company but if the company doesn't fit who you are, there are another 1,000 out there that might be a much better place to thrive."

- Luigi Matrone, Founder & CEO of E-Business Institute

"I love desire. The burning in one's gut to win. I can teach 90% of what a person needs to win in business but I can't teach desire. That has to come from within."

- James Lafferty, CEO of British American Tobacco Philippines

"Work hard, play hard. Work is important but do not forget that we work to live – not the reverse."

- Michel Lambert, Global Director Media Planning & Operations at Procter & Gamble

"Show a mix of hunger and true grit when it gets really tough. Never accept that the vision is impossible and chase every chance to achieve it!"

- **Michelle Crossan, Vice-President for Strategy & Transformation at Samsung Europe**

"Life is short. If you're lucky enough to not live in a place where you have to fight for survival – do what you love for a living.

- **Michel Jouveaux, Founder, Composer & Musician at SoundAdvice, Marketing Consultant at Idea Bakery**

WILL YOU DO US A FAVOUR?

If you enjoyed *How to Succeed in Your First Job*, would you mind taking a minute to write a review on Amazon? Even a short review helps and it would mean a lot to us.

If a friend is also just starting, or has started, their first job, why not share the Amazon book page with them to give them a head start on their career as well?

Finally don't forget that you can find more resources on our website **www.wolfleaders.com**. You can also follow us on Twitter **@wolfleaderspack** or on Facebook **Wolf Leaders Academy**. Use the hashtag **#GetAheadOfThePack** to comment on the book!

We wish you the best of luck in your first job – and beyond!

Anna and Serena

FURTHER READING

Hungry for more? Here are some of the books that we've read and found particularly insightful when it comes to working efficiently and effectively and developing into the leaders we aspire to be.

David Allen, *Getting Things Done: Stress-Free Productivity*

Kenneth Blanchard and Spencer Johnson, *The One-Minute Manager*

Dale Carnegie, *How to Win Friends and Influence People*

Jim Collins, *Good to Great*

Stephen R. Covey, *The 7 Habits of Highly Effective People: Powerful Lessons in Personal Change*

Simon Sinek, *Start with Why: How Great Leaders Inspire Everyone to Take Action*

Michael Watkins, *First 90 Days: Critical Success Strategies for New Leaders at All Levels*

ACKNOWLEDGEMENTS

We would like to thank all our friends and colleagues who have contributed their insights and personal stories to this book. We are incredibly touched that so many of you have been willing to share your experiences and advice to help a new generation of managers to succeed in their careers.

We also want to thank our own managers and mentors who have helped us on our leadership journeys so far.

ABOUT THE AUTHORS

Serena De Maio, serena@wolfleaders.com
Lead Trainer, **Wolf Leaders Academy**
Entrepreneur & Co-founder, **Grace & Wilde**
Twitter: @serena_demaio

Previously Greater Europe Business Intelligence Leader at Procter & Gamble, Serena combines expertise in both brand management and operational marketing. Her 15 years of work experience span from beauty to fashion, restaurants, retail, and the entertainment industry. In parallel to her successful corporate career, she has co-founded Grace & Wilde Luxury Shapewear and Wolf Leaders Academy. Serena also coaches early stage startups, writes about leadership, startups and brand management, and is an international conference speaker.

Serena is a tough but fair leader; she's direct, and likes to push the boundaries of political correctness.

People who have worked with Serena say:

"Serena is a highly skilled, effective & efficient manager, who gets the absolute best out of her team. She has consistently encouraged & inspired me to grow, learn, and be the best I can be."

"She raises team motivation to the next level. Very inspiring, always two steps ahead with marketing innovations [...] a great leader."

"I encourage you to listen to what she has to say, as she's usually right!"

Anna Lundberg, anna@wolfleaders.com
Lead Trainer, **Wolf Leaders Academy**
Director & Consultant, **Crocus Communications**
Personal Coach, **One Step Outside**
Twitter: @annaselundberg

Anna is a personal coach and business consultant. After a successful marketing career at Procter & Gamble, she has since worked independently with clients including Burberry, Vertu, IBM, and increasingly also small businesses and startups. Today, she mentors entrepreneurs and young managers via Virgin Starts-up, Seedcamp, and Clarity, while she juggles her own three businesses.

Anna is a constant self-improver, ever curious, ever learning. She devours books on business, leadership and effectiveness, always looking for ways in which to optimise the way she organises her work and her life.

People who have worked with Anna say:

"Anna is fantastic – smart, creative [...] both strategic and pragmatic."

"Her knowledge mixed with great collaboration skills made her a great coach and trainer, both for our agencies and ourselves."

"If you need a digital expert, branding expert and a great thought leader then Anna is the person for you."

Made in the USA
San Bernardino, CA
29 November 2019